Through Cancer God Showed Me Mercy

Mini Writings of the Bipolar Mind

Elizabeth Spencer

ISBN-13: 9798672390857
ISBN-10: 1477123456

Cover design by: Art Painter
Library of Congress Control Number: 2018675309
Printed in the United States of America

I truly must dedicate this book to my own personal hummingbird. My mother.

Alice Spencer

You have always been my strength. Seeing everything you have gone thru and still find a way to see the greatness in this world. You truly are an amazing woman. I love you to the moon and back.

Humble & Flow Enterprise

Author: Elizabeth Spencer

Table of Content

Covid-19

I thought it was all working the way it was supposed to. I had a job. Was able to go to the gym. Got my apartment. I was starting to rebuild myself again. This time for me. Struggling with mental illness and not knowing how to express my emotions. I struggled for years thinking I was unloved and unwanted.

While thinking my plan was on the right path, covid-19 shut the world down. So much uncertainly and fear cast all over the nations. So many people lost jobs and true hope.

We became trapped inside ourselves. At least, I know for me, every-thing crumbled inside my head. Already fighting being angry with God. I wanted things my way. Was so blind with my own generational hatred, I didn't see the blessings God kept shoving in my face. I took it all for granted. So, now the world closed. God made sure to pay our bills though. He took that stress from us.

During this time, I'm dealing with my mom having just been diagnosed with lung cancer. She took chemo and radiation. Plus has M.S. (multiple sclerosis), degenerative disk disease. She has a metal plate in her neck and metal bars in her back.

I couldn't see I was blessed to not worry about bills and be there for my family. Honor thy mother. I felt burdened by this. I couldn't let all my emotions go from my past. I wrestled with seeing the blessings and trying to deny them and make excuses. I see now, I've witnessed so much since I was small. Had taken so much pain and still just wanted to love. God's grace truly has brought me this far. But again, I was blinded by my own thoughts and fear.

From my upbringing, I was so guarded. Which also turned me more masculine personality wise and extremely stubborn.
By the merciful grace of God,
I was truly broken down to be
molded to show His love.

Because I was so hardheaded and stubborn; God sent His soldier to wake me up. Remember, I said I had turned manly in my personality. Tried to be Alpha.

I'm sure God had to be laughing at my crazy self. He showed me. God loves us so much; He sends who we need to open our eyes.

I can only say, I wish I would have seen it a more peaceful way. I fought all the wrong way. So much blood, tears, and pain that was unnecessary.

Proverbs 3: 5-6

Trust in the Lord with all
thine heart; and lean not unto
thine own understanding. In
all ways acknowledge him, and
he shall direct thy paths.

Saving Grace

Because I pushed everyone out of my life by trying to be in charge. God sent a warrior to show me a better way. I can never say thank you enough, for choking the air out of me, so God could blow His love and grace into me, and open my eyes. Without that; I would have missed so much.

I was able to spend so much time with my mom. Going to doctors, shopping, eating. This wonderful woman who is always with a smile and such childlike joy to give to the world.

I was worrying about what? Mad

for what? This lady I'm spending all this time with. Always laughing and wanted to give. Is medically going through so much but was so happy when she was just able to eat at one of her favorite restaurants.

She has always been my rock. As I've told her. I've gotten my strength by watching her. I forgot to remember to appreciate the small things. I feel so much honor that I was able to be there for my mother. She has always been there for me no matter what.

I can say, I'd be a fool, not to follow God's way. After the true miracles' I've seen. I know His love is real and it does give peace to the soul!

2 Peter 1: 2

Grace and peace be multiplied unto you through the knowledge of God, and of Jesus our Lord.

Hebrews 4: 16

Let us then approach the throne
of Grace with confidence, so that we
may receive mercy and find grace
to help us in our time of need.

A Dreamers Thoughts

Hummingbird

Hummingbirds are so small but such an immense part of this world. If they all went away we would have nectar-producing plants go extinct.

The biblical meaning for them is a creature that trieds to bring happiness. They solidify the symbolism of eternity, continuity, and infinity. The hummingbird is tireless in its pursuit for finding sweetness.

As my mother is like the hummingbird. We all need to be tireless in our pursuit for God's love. If we just take the time to stop our busy lives. Just enjoy the little moments God allows us. Even just a smile can be so life changing for someone. We all need to be hummingbirds of Christ. Spread joy and love all over the globe.

I urge you to follow us on Instagram. With our Suicide Watch Program, we are also here for anyone who needs us. Even if it's just a shoulder to cry on and a listening ear. God loves all and we are here to show His love.

Danny, Humble G, Jefferies

thegluepodcastshow@instagram

Elizabeth Spencer

Elizaard69@instagram
icegemlizzard@gmail.com

Notes